The Osage Indian Murders: The History of the Notorious Killing Spree and the Federal Investigations in the Early 20th Century

By Charles River Editors

FEAR OF KILLERS FILLS OSAGE WITH WHISPERS

Three victims of the Osage murder ring. Above, Henry Roan, Indian on whose murder the indictment against William K. Hale is based. At right, above, is Reta Smith, Indian ,who was mysteriously killed, and, below, Henry Vaughn, white lawyer who was killed because he knew too much about the murder of a certain Indian.

did anything about it. The Osage people were not surprised by the revelations of the federal investi...

Henry Roan, Rita Smith, and William Vaughn

About Charles River Editors

Charles River Editors provides superior editing and original writing services across the digital publishing industry, with the expertise to create digital content for publishers across a vast range of subject matter. In addition to providing original digital content for third party publishers, we also republish civilization's greatest literary works, bringing them to new generations of readers via ebooks.

Sign up here to receive updates about free books as we publish them, and visit Our Kindle Author Page to browse today's free promotions and our most recently published Kindle titles.

Introduction

Important Figures in Osage Murder Case

INCOME
$135.000
PER YEAR

MOLLIE
BURKHART

"BILLY"
HALE

A 1926 cartoon depicting Mollie Burkhart and William Hale

Throughout the 19th century, the people of the Osage Nation, like many other Native American groups, were forced to relocate from their traditional tribal lands to "Indian Territory," land set aside as reservations by the federal government. The Osage shared this unincorporated territory with other tribes, including the Cherokee, Seminole, Choctaw,

Chickasaw, and Creek.

In the late 19th century, Indian Territory became part of the new State of Oklahoma and tribal lands were gradually reduced in size, but on some of the lands assigned to the Osage, which became Osage County, something very dramatic happened: oil was discovered. At first, that didn't seem too important - in the 1880s, oil was useful but wasn't the source of wealth it would later become. However, the rise of the automobile changed everything. In 1900, there were only around 4,000 automobiles registered in America, but by 1908, there were over 60,000, and by the early 1920s, there were over 15 million. Every single one needed fuel and lubricants that came from oil, and as a result, "black gold" became one of the most valuable commodities on Earth.

For the Osage, the explosion in demand for oil brought unimaginable wealth. In 1923 alone, the Osage Nation received over $30 million in oil revenue, worth over $400 million in current value, and individual members of the tribe became extremely wealthy. Unscrupulous people began to plot how they could get their hands on some of this wealth.

Then the murders began.

In the early 1920s, members of the Osage Nation and others began to turn up dead, and in many cases, the proceeds of oil revenue owned by these people passed to white "Guardians" appointed by the federal government. By 1925, at least 24 Osage had died in unexplained circumstances, and some accounts suggest that the actual number may have been over 100. Local law enforcement seemed unable (or perhaps unwilling) to investigate effectively, and it was left to a small bureau in Washington to undertake their first homicide investigation under the leadership of a dynamic and ambitious young lawyer named J. Edgar Hoover. As a result, the horrifying true story of the Osage County murders became one of the first assignments for the federal agency that would later become the FBI.

The Osage Indian Murders: The History of the Notorious Killing Spree and the Federal Investigations in the Early 20th Century

The Osage and Oil

During much of the 19th century, the relationships between the federal government and Native Americans were characterized by hardships and unremitting violence. After victory in the American Revolution in 1783, American settlers began to relentlessly expand across the territories they occupied to the west of the original 13 colonies. The only thing that stood in their way were the Native Americans who already lived there. There were frequent small-scale conflicts between white settlers and Native Americans until, in 1830, President Andrew Jackson signed into law the Indian Removal Act. On the surface, the law may have sounded relatively innocuous, proposing an "exchange of lands" with Native Americans, but in reality, the legislation allowed state-sponsored ethnic cleansing as tribes were forcibly relocated from their lands and forced to more to "Indian Territory", an area of land defined by the Nonintercourse Act of 1834 in present-day Kansas Oklahoma. These forced relocations were undertaken with great brutality and in appalling weather, and on the Trail of Tears, at least 3,000

Native Americans died as they were forced out of their homelands.

The Osage probably originated, like many other Dhegiha Sioux tribes, near the mouth of the Green River in present-day Kentucky. By the 1830s, Osage tribes occupied territory in what is now Missouri, Oklahoma, and Arkansas, but under the Indian Removal Act, all were forced to move to an area near the Verdigris River in the Indian Territory. In 1871, the 3,000 remaining Osage were once again forced to move, this time to another part of Indian Territory in present-day north-central Oklahoma. Again, this move was enforced in a way that killed many Osage on the way.

The new lands on which the Osage were forced to settle comprised almost 1.5 million acres and were formally recognized as the Osage Reservation by an Act of Congress in 1874. As with most reservations, this land was treated as sovereign territory over which the federal government had no direct jurisdiction, and, in this case, the Osage were able to raise sufficient funds to legally purchase this land. That would become very important decades later.

Few Native American groups had the funds to purchase their reservation lands, which meant the federal government was able to gradually take away portions of their lands for white settlers. Since they were the legal owners of their own lands, that would never happen to the Osage.

Communications between members of the Osage and the federal government were conducted via the Osage Agency, a part of the federal Bureau of Indian Affairs (BIA), with its headquarters at Deep Ford on Bird Creek, (present-day Pawhuska, Oklahoma).

For the Osage (and for most Native Americans forced into reservations), life was tough. Unable to follow their traditional ways of life on unfamiliar and poor lands, there were few opportunities for the Osage, and many lived in poverty. Then, in 1894, white men began to arrive on the Osage Reservation looking for something completely unexpected: oil.

During the previous decades in America, new technologies had brought about all kinds of industrial changes. The development of steam engines brought industrialization and an increasing demand for coal and for products derived from coal, including "coal oil," used for lubrication and to provide fuel for lamps. However, by the late 19th century, coal was becoming increasingly scarce and expensive to extract, so there was an ongoing search for new forms of fuel and lubricant.

Crude oil, which seeps to the surface in many places in the United States, had long been recognized as a source of medicines used for treating rheumatism and sprains, but by the end of the 19th century, it was recognized that this naturally occurring substance could be refined to create new products that might replace those that had previously come from coal. In 1859, a man named Edwin Drake, working on behalf of the world's first oil company, the Pennsylvania Rock Oil Company, drilled the world's first oil well in Pennsylvania and began to extract crude oil from huge underground reservoirs. The oil was refined to produce kerosene, and it became a cleaner and cheaper alternative to coal oil.

Drake

At this point, oil wasn't yet a high-value commodity and demand was relatively limited, but in 1894, prospectors began looking at the prairies of the Osage Reservation as another potential source of crude oil. Early exploration suggested that parts of Osage County might be located on vast underground reservoirs of oil, so in 1897, the Phoenix Oil Company established the first commercial oil well on the reservation, though this was tiny compared to those that would follow, producing just 20 barrels of crude oil each day. The rights to drill for oil on the reservation had been agreed to with the Osage Tribal Council, but, given that each barrel produced from this first well sold for just $1, and the Osage received commission of 10% on each barrel sold, the revenue that was generated was initially very modest.[1]

In 1905, Oklahoma Territory and Indian Territory were merged and became the 46th state in the United States as Oklahoma. Negotiations began to change the Osage Reservation into Osage County, and during these negotiations, the Osage Tribal Council was able to secure an agreement that the members of the tribe would retain the mineral rights on the former reservation lands. However, while individuals could own certain pieces of land, the mineral rights would be communal and any revenue they generated would be distributed equally amongst the Osage. To the federal government, this probably didn't seem to be a major factor, because in 1906, when the agreement was signed, oil still wasn't particularly valuable and the wells operating

---

[1] From Osage County website, retrieved from https://osage.okcounties.org/about, October 2023.

at that time were still not generating a great deal of revenue. Agreeing that the Osage could keep the mineral rights to their land didn't seem like a major concession given that nobody understood the land would generate a great deal of money.

However, soon after, a technological revolution swept America and the rest of the world, and the demand for oil – along with its price – rose exponentially. The first internal combustion engines were developed in the last decades of the 19th century, and they initially used a volatile hydrocarbon obtained from coal gas for fuel, but this fuel was expensive and difficult to produce. By the end of the 19th century, a new fuel had been developed for internal combustion engines: gasoline, derived by refining crude oil. The availability of this new, cleaner, and inexpensive fuel prompted further development of internal combustion engines and vehicles that used gas as a power source.

In 1900, there were around 8,000 registered automobiles and trucks in the United States, and all of them required gasoline as fuel. Just as the Osage were signing an agreement with the federal government, demand for vehicles (and the gasoline needed to power them) began to increase at unprecedented rates. By 1910, there were over half a million registered vehicles on the roads of America, and by 1914, the Ford Motor Company alone was producing more than half a million Model T automobiles each year. By 1919, there were over 8 million registered vehicles in the United States, and demand was only continuing to grow.

As more cars took to the roads, demand for gasoline increased vastly. By 1919, America was producing over 350 million barrels of oil each year, and that still wasn't enough to keep pace with growing demand. In a short space of time, crude oil and the products derived from it became some of the most important and valuable resources in the world.

Surveying indicated that there were vast oil reserves under parts of north-central Oklahoma, particularly under the lands owned by the Osage. Based on the seemingly unending demand for more oil products, the Osage Tribal Council began to hold auctions for the rights to drill for oil on their land.

These auctions, held four times each year, were overseen by officials from the Department of the Interior, and representatives from existing and new oil companies came to bid for drilling rights that might prove to be extremely lucrative. In fine weather, the auctions were held in the open air on Ki-He-Kah Hill near a large elm tree outside the town of Pawhuska, now the administrative center of Osage County. Vast amounts were bid for the most promising sites for drilling, and in the press, these were avidly covered, to the extent that the tree under which they took place became known as the "Million Dollar Elm." When it had first granted drilling rights on its land to oil companies, the Osage Tribal Council had asked for only $100 for each new well. After the auctions began, prices climbed rapidly, and one of the most promising sites was leased for a then record-breaking $2 million. By 1907, Oklahoma was producing more crude oil than any other state.

Under the terms of the agreement with the federal government, the Osage Tribal Council had agreed that individual Osage property owners would not be able to negotiate separately with oil companies.

Instead, the mineral rights in Osage County were defined as communal, so that they would be negotiated by members of the tribal council and the revenues would be distributed equally as royalties amongst members of the tribes. But as the oil auctions under the elm tree began to bring in more and more cash, some of the Osage became vastly wealthy almost overnight.

Each one of the 2,229 Osage on the tribal rolls in 1907 received "headrights," the right to receive a quarterly payment that represented a share of the oil revenue generated from tribal lands. These people were also permitted to vote in tribal elections. Any money paid by an oil company for drilling rights was placed in a trust administered by the BIA, which was also responsible for overseeing the payment of revenues to headright holders. Headrights could not be bought or sold, but they could be inherited.

In 1916, the average headright quarterly payment was worth around $1,250. To put that in perspective, over half of workers in the United States at that time earned less than $2,000 per year.

And as demand for oil increased, headright payments also increased, to the point that in 1920, the average quarterly headright payment had risen to around $37,000, and in 1923, headrights peaked at an average quarterly payment of over $50,000. The Osage, or at least, those who possessed headrights, suddenly found themselves with amounts of money that would have been inconceivable to the average American.

Members of the Osage tribe began to spend the money that suddenly began to flow into their hands through headright payments. Many purchased large, ostentatious houses, as well as automobiles. Some bought more than one of each - one newspaper reported that on average, one in every 11 people in America owned an automobile by the early 1920s, whereas in Osage County, on average, each individual owned 11 automobiles. That wasn't true, nor were stories that members of the tribe abandoned automobiles and purchased new ones if they had a flat tire, but these exaggerated reports were widely believed, as was the assertion that members of the Osage had become, due to oil payments, the wealthiest social group per capita in the world.[2]

To many Americans struggling just to get by, it seemed unfair that this small group of Native Americans had suddenly become enormously wealthy and were able to take foreign holidays, buy cars, fancy clothes, and in some cases send their children to expensive private schools. Some people felt jealousy or resentment that what appeared to be nothing more than luck had suddenly given the Osage more wealth than most ordinary people would see in a lifetime. Newspaper stories reflected these feelings. *The Travel Magazine* published an article on Osage County that claimed, "The Osage Indian is today the prince of spendthrifts." Another report, featured in *Harper's Monthly Magazine* raised a particular concern, telling readers, "Every time a new well is drilled the Indians are that much richer. The Osage Indians are becoming so rich that something will have to be done about it." The notion that "something will have to be done about it" became common outside Osage County.[3]

[2] GeoExPro website, *Oil Wealth and the Osage Murders*, retrieved from https://geoexpro.com/oil-wealth-and-the-osage-murders/ October 2023.

[3] Library of Congress, *The Osage in Historic Newspapers: Envy, Ridicule and Racism*, retrieved from

It didn't matter that this was the "Roaring Twenties," a period of conspicuous consumption during which rapid social and technological changes made businessmen and speculators multi-millionaires who spent on a vast scale (and often unwisely). Perhaps nothing typified this accumulation of wealth more clearly than when J.P. Morgan died in 1913. Morgan had been one of America's leading financiers, but upon hearing that Morgan's estate was worth $80 million, his friend and colleague John D. Rockefeller was said to have remarked; "And to think he wasn't even a wealthy man!"

When the people accumulating wealth were white, that seemed to be acceptable, but when Native Americans suddenly became wealthy and began flaunting that wealth through lavish spending, that was clearly not acceptable. Plenty of Americans seemed to regard them as naïve and incapable of dealing rationally with the sudden acquisition of wealth. One person appointed by the BOI to help the Osage spend their money wisely remarked that most

https://blogs.loc.gov/headlinesandheroes/2021/11/the-osage-in-historic-newspapers-envy-ridicule-and-racism/ October 2023.

Native Americans were "like a child six or eight years old."

Guardians

In 1908, when headright payments first began to amount to more than a few dollars, Congress gave the power to county probate courts in Oklahoma to appoint a white guardian to help manage the financial affairs of any member of the Osage if that person was judged to be "incompetent" or too young to manage their own financial affairs. In practice, the decision as to whether a person was "incompetent" was decided by the Department of the Interior, acting through the BIA, and it was hardly a coincidence that the people most likely to be defined in this way were full-blooded Native Americans. Those of mixed race were rarely considered to be in need of the services of a white guardian.

However, even this system did not satisfy many people, and soon, Congress began to scrutinize the financial affairs of the Osage. Inspectors were sent to Osage County to find out what was happening and report back to Congress. At a House subcommittee meeting in 1920, a report from one of these inspectors was carefully examined. It asserted, "Every white man in Osage County will tell you that the Indians are now running wild. The day has come when we must begin our restriction of these moneys or dismiss from our hearts and conscience any hope we have of building the Osage Indian into a true citizen.[4]"

On March 3, 1921, Congress passed a new law mandating a federal guardianship system. This contained a wholly new approach and one under which the government no longer had to prove that a member of the Osage was incompetent in order to prevent them from managing their own finances. Instead, it became the responsibility of individual Osage members under the age of 21 and/or of full or half Native American blood to prove their own competence. If they failed to do this, their affairs would be managed by a white guardian appointed by the government. This was a breathtaking piece of legislation and one that, had it been applied to white people, would have generated understandable outrage and protest. However, since it was directed

---

[4] Cited in David Grann, *Killers of the Flower Moon: The Osage Murders and the Birth of the FBI*, 2017.

at a relatively small number of Native Americans, it was passed into law with little debate.

It seems likely that many of the legislators truly believed that this was in the best interests of the Osage. This paternalistic view of their duty of protection towards Native Americans was clearly underwritten by racial prejudice and stereotypes that saw Native Americans as being less intelligent than white people and fundamentally incapable of managing their own affairs effectively.

Under the new law, strict limits were placed on how much each member of the Osage could withdraw from their headright trust fund in each financial year, and before long, more than 600 state and federally appointed white guardians were operating in Osage County to oversee the headright trust funds of a large number of Osage. Depriving people of access to funds to which they had a legal and moral right has no parallel in American history – the Osage were simply treated like foolish children who had to be protected from their own naivety and lack of financial understanding, despite the fact that prior to 1921, there was no shortage of evidence that many Osage had invested their headright payments in sensible and prudent ways.

At the same time, the law passed by Congress in 1921 was open to manipulation and fraud. Not only did it take away from many Osage the right to manage their own finances, it also inadvertently created a situation where unscrupulous white guardians could expropriate money arriving in the headright trust funds. State courts, mainly run by white lawyers, appointed guardians, who were mostly white lawyers. Once these guardians had been appointed by a court, there was no fixed limit on the administration charges they could take, so many were able to take fees from the trust funds that were, at the very least, extremely high. There was also some question surrounding whether the Osage were actually entitled to any quarterly headright payments that exceeded $1,000. From 1921-1924, headright payments were well above this level, and some guardians took the view that they had the right to keep any payments to trust funds over this value. Given that there was no form of oversight or accounting on the actions of guardians, many snatched the opportunity to enrich themselves at the expense of the people they were ostensibly supposed to be representing. A government study in 1924[5] estimated that from 1921-1924, the white guardians in Osage County took for themselves through excessive administration charges and "surplus" headright payments somewhere in the region of $8 million, worth about $150 million today. Several Osage who should have received tens of thousands of dollars in headright payments instead found themselves in debt, often to their unscrupulous guardians.

The ways in which white people in Osage County were able to help themselves to money that clearly belonged to the Osage finally prompted Congress to investigate the actions of guardians in 1924. However, by that time it had become apparent that the law passed by Congress in 1921 had more sinister implications. For example, if a man married an Osage woman who was entitled to a headright payment and that woman died, then her husband inherited the rights to the headright payments. If an Osage for whom a white guardian was acting died,

[5] Cited in Dennis McAuliffe, *Bloodland: A Family Story of Oil, Greed and Murder on the Osage Reservation*, 1999.

then in some circumstances, the guardian could inherit that person's headright payments.

In other words, the new law had established a situation whereby the death of an Osage could make white guardians and others very wealthy, and perhaps not so coincidentally, starting around 1921, dozens of members of the Osage tribe began to turn up dead under very suspicious circumstances.

The Osage Indian Murders

In the early 20th century, William King Hale was one of the most successful white businessmen in Osage County. He owned a 5,000-acre ranch as well as part shares in the general store and funeral home in the town of Fairfax, where he also held a controlling interest in the town's only bank. He was also a Deputy Sheriff in Fairfax, and he declared himself to be a friend of the Osage. At some point around 1920, he began to call himself "King of the Osage Hills."

Hale

In 1917, Hale's nephew, Ernest Burkhart, married Mollie Kyle, a full-blood Osage. Interracial marriage was uncommon at the time and generally frowned upon amongst whites, and many took to contemptuously calling Ernest "squaw man". However, Mollie owned a full headright, as did several other members of her immediate family. In May 1921, Mollie became worried about her sister, 34-year-old Anna Brown, who had disappeared. Anna had last been seen when she went to Fairfax with Mollie's husband, Ernest Burkhart, and with his brothers Bryan and Horace. Bryan Burkhart said that he had dropped Anna at her home at around 5:00 p.m., and that was the last time that any member of the family saw her alive. Anna had a history of drinking, so most people seemed to assume that she had gone off on a spree, but Mollie wasn't so sure.

Around a week later, a man and two boys out squirrel-hunting near a small creek found the decomposing body of Anna Brown, and the undertaker who examined the body determined that she had been shot in the back of the head. An investigation by local law enforcement made little progress, so the conclusion reached in July 1921 was that Anna had been murdered for reasons unknown by unidentified killers. With that, the case was closed.

Anna had owned a headright, and upon her death, it passed to Mollie. This wasn't the first additional headright that Mollie had received, as her younger sister, 27-year-old Minnie, had died three years earlier from what doctors had described as a "peculiar wasting illness." There had been whispers of poisoning, but nothing had been proved.

Mollie's mother, Lizzie Q. Kyle, became ill soon after Anna's death. Doctors were unable to say precisely what it was she was suffering from, but her health declined steadily until her death in late July 1921. Lizzie had owned three headrights, and these too passed to Mollie after her mother's death. Some people, including Mollie's brother-in-law, Bill Smith, were convinced that Lizzie had been poisoned, but there was no direct evidence to support the theory. Bill Smith undertook his own efforts to investigate but made little progress. He and his wife became convinced that strangers were approaching their house at night, and they began to fear for their own safety. They moved abruptly into a new house in hopes of escaping the night-time intruders, but they continued to be troubled by strange noises outside, as if people were surreptitiously prowling around the new house.

In March 1923, an explosion ripped through the Smith's new home, killing Bill Smith, his wife Rita (Mollie's last surviving sister), and Nettie

Brookshire, a 19-year-old white maid. The explosion was clearly caused by a bomb, and local newspapers carried outraged editorials demanding that the people behind the bombing be found and convicted, but local law enforcement failed to find the perpetrator, or even a viable suspect.[6]

In any criminal investigation, and especially a murder investigation, the first principal is establishing a motive, often by figuring out who would benefit from the crime. The deaths of Mollie Kyle's family members meant that she received several headrights that were worth, collectively, millions of dollars. However, if she died (and she had become intermittently ill after her mother's death with a similarly inexplicable illness), then her husband, Ernest Burkhart (one of the last people to see Anna alive), would inherit all these headrights. To many people, it seemed apparent that the spate of unexplained murders in Osage County was connected to headright payments, but there were concerns that local law enforcement officials were too closely connected to the legal and justice

[6] FBI website, *Osage Murders Case*, retrieved from https://www.fbi.gov/history/famous-cases/osage-murders-case October 2023.

systems (and many headright guardians were lawyers) to be able to conduct an unbiased investigation.

In April 1923, in direct response to mounting public concern, Oklahoma Governor Jack C. Walton ordered the senior state investigator, a former private detective named Herman Fox Davis, to go to Osage County and find out what was happening. However, Davis' investigation didn't exactly go well - he appeared to spend most of his time in Osage County in saloons drinking, often with the very people he was supposed to be investigating. In June, Davis was found guilty of accepting bribes and was given a two-year prison sentence. Soon after, he was pardoned by the governor, but within months, Davis was found guilty of the murder and robbery of an attorney and given a life sentence. In November, Governor Walton was impeached and removed from office after it was discovered that he had received a number of substantial payments, some from oil barons involved in drilling in Osage County.

Walton

Thankfully, not all investigators in Osage County were as inept and corrupt as Herman Davis. In August 1922, a 55-year-old wealthy white oilman who lived in Osage County, Barney McBride, had become concerned about the wave of unexplained deaths in the area. He told friends that he planned to travel to Washington to meet with contacts in the government and urge them to start a federal investigation.

He arrived in Washington and checked into a

rooming house, only to vanish the same evening. The following morning, his body was discovered in a ditch in Maryland. He had been brutally beaten, his skull was crushed, and he had been stabbed more than 20 times. His murderer was never identified.[7]

McBride's death underscored that whatever was happening in Osage County wasn't just lethal for those who owned headrights, and this became even more clear in the case of a former public prosecutor and attorney who lived in Pawhuska, W.W. Vaughan, who had spoken publicly about not just the murders in Osage County but also about the guardians' corruption, bribery, and graft. In June 1923, Vaughan received a telephone call from a friend of George Bigheart, a member of the Osage and the owner of a headright, after Bigheart had suddenly and mysteriously become seriously ill. The friend suspected poisoning, and Bigheart wanted to tell what he knew about what was really happening in Osage County. He had read Vaugan's statements about corruption in the local press and wanted to make a statement to the attorney. Vaughan went to

[7] University of Tulsa, *TU Professor Bailey's work assists New York Times' best-selling author David Grann*, retrieved from https://utulsa.edu/david-grann-garrick-bailey/ October 2023.

the hospital in Oklahoma City to which Bigheart had been admitted after he fell ill, and he spent several hours alone with Bigheart before the man died.

Vaughan planned to take an overnight train to return to Pawhuska, but before boarding the train, he made a telephone call that would ultimately prove fatal. He called the Sheriff of Osage County and told him that he had evidence not just that George Bigheart had been murdered, but about a web of corruption and murder that had spread across the county. Vaughan boarded the train in Oklahoma City, but when it arrived in Pawhuska, there was no sign of the attorney. His clothes and luggage were found in a sleeping compartment, but Vaughan wasn't on the train and none of the other passengers could say what had happened to him. Two days later, his naked body was found next to the railroad line north of Oklahoma City. His neck had been broken, and the working assumption was that he had been hurled from the speeding train. Before leaving to visit the hospital in Oklahoma City, Vaughan had told his wife that he had amassed a collection of documents that detailed his knowledge of the Osage

County murders, and that he had hidden the papers and told his wife where they could be found if anything happened to him. When the place he had identified was searched, there was nothing there – it seemed someone had found the cache of incriminating documents and removed them.

These murders made it very clear that something nefarious was happening in Osage County, but as it turned out, these murders were just the beginning of what would become known as the "reign of terror."

On the same day that the body of Anna Brown was found by squirrel hunters, an oil worker made an equally gruesome discovery. Stepping away from a drilling derrick near the town of Pawhuska for a cigarette, he noticed something partially hidden in low brush, and when he looked closer, he found that it was a decomposing human body. Investigators discovered that this was the body of Charles Whitehorn, a member of the Osage (and a cousin of Mollie Burkhart) who owned a headright. He had been shot twice in the head at close range, but yet again, an investigation by the authorities failed to find any motive or a viable suspect. Just like the death of Anna Brown, this was classified as a killing by a person, or persons, unknown. Nine months later, Osage County Sheriff Harve Freas was expelled after having been found guilty of failing to uphold the law.

All the while, the murders continued. In February 1922, a member of the Osage, 29-year-old William Stepson, received a telephone call at his house in Fairfax. He didn't tell his wife who had called, but he said that he would have to leave immediately for an important meeting. When he returned home several hours later, he was seriously ill, and he died a short time later. An investigation surmised that he had met with someone who had given him poison in some form, and that it rapidly killed him. No suspects were identified, and no motive for his murder was discovered.

About a month later, an Osage woman died suddenly from an unidentified and very sudden illness. Members of her family suspected poisoning, but no toxicology examination of her body was carried out and no investigation followed. On July 28, 1922, an Osage man, 30-year-old Joe Bates, was given a drink of whisky by an unidentified stranger. Bates collapsed soon after, foaming at the mouth and having difficulty breathing. Within hours, he too was dead. This time, there was no doubt that he had been poisoned, but an investigation failed to identify the man who had given him the whisky, and the case was closed without any suspects being named.

In February 1923, hunters spotted a Buick car seemingly abandoned in a rocky valley not far from Fairfax. When they looked inside, they found a man slumped behind the wheel. A deputy sheriff from Fairfax and the town marshal were summoned, and they determined that the body in the car was that of an Osage man, 40-year-old Henry Roan. He had been killed by a single shot to the back of the head. It was revealed that the dead man was in some financial difficulty due to problems with headright payments and had turned to his best friend, William King Hale (Mollie Burkhart's father-in-law), for help. Hale explained that he had given Roan a number of informal loans, and that was why Roan had named Hale as the sole beneficiary on a life insurance policy worth $25,000 that Roan had taken out a short time before his murder. It also turned out that, many years before, Roan had briefly been married to Mollie Burkhart, though the two seemed to have parted on good terms.

Naturally, the series of murders caused a wave of fear amongst the Osage. Electric light was still a novelty in rural areas in 1923, but many of the Osage used their headright payments to pay for their homes to be connected to the electric supply, and many mounted lights outside their house. These were left burning all night. Some whites thought this was just one more ostentatious display of wealth from people who had more money than sense, but for the Osage, the fear of unknown intruders outside their homes was very real and very pervasive. In fact, reporters began to refer to this time in Osage County as the "reign of terror".

What made the situation worse for the Osage was that local law enforcement and the justice system seemed to offer no help. Nobody had been arrested for any of the murders, despite the fact that at least two dozen people had died in Osage County, and there weren't even any acknowledged suspects. The local justice of the peace, the person responsible for convening inquests into these deaths, had himself received death threats and frankly admitted that he was too afraid to hold inquests into the latest murders. The new sheriff also said, much later, that he too had received threats that made him wary of conducting effective investigations, admitting, "I didn't want to get mixed up in it."[8] Needless to say, that was a frank and frightening admission from the man responsible for the investigation of crime in Osage County.

In desperation, members of the Osage Tribal Council decided to turn to the federal government for help. After the bombing that killed Bill and Rita Smith in March 1923, the tribal council passed a formal resolution in which it noted that it was "essential for the preservation of the lives and property of members of the tribe that prompt and strenuous action be taken to capture and punish the criminals." A copy of this resolution, which also included an appeal that the Department of Justice become involved, was sent to the only US Senator

---

[8] Cited in Dennis McAuliffe, *Bloodland: A Family Story of Oil, Greed and Murder on the Osage Reservation*, 1999.

who also had Native American ancestry, Charles Curtis, a representative from Kansas.

Curtis

Soon after, Curtis approached the Department of Justice. It was very clear that law and order had completely broken down in Osage County, and local law enforcement seemed unable to take effective action. Some kind of federal intervention was clearly needed.

The Bureau of Investigation

Until 1908, there was no federal investigative

agency in the United States. Law enforcement was carried out by police departments in large cities and by sheriff's departments in rural areas. The US Marshals Service had been founded back in 1789, but in the early years of the 20th century, this service was mainly used to protect members of the judiciary, serve warrants and subpoenas, and, where required, assist in hunts for known criminals. The members of this service were not trained or experienced in detection or in carrying out investigations to identify criminals.

In 1896, National Chiefs of Police Union founded the National Bureau of Criminal Identification, an organization charged with maintaining files that could help state law enforcement to identify criminals who operated across state lines, but this wasn't a federal organization. It would not be until 1908 that President Theodore Roosevelt ordered Attorney General Charles Bonaparte to create a new federal body that would maintain special agents and be capable of undertaking investigation of criminal cases. In part, the new organization was founded in response to the assassination of President William McKinley in 1901 by anarchist Leon Czolgosz.

There were fears that anarchists might pose a threat to the political stability of America.

The new agency, the Bureau of Investigation (BOI), would report only and directly to the Attorney General, but in its early days, there was a great deal of doubt about just what the BOI was supposed to do. Just 34 BOI "special agents," many of whom were former members of the Secret Service, were appointed and undertook a number of investigations into anarchists and other political groups suspected of being involved in terrorism, as well as organized prostitution gangs, the so-called "white slave trade."

In 1919 a dynamic, mercurial, and ambitious 24-year-old lawyer, John Edgar Hoover, was appointed to head the General Intelligence Division of the BOI, the division charged with monitoring suspect political groups in the United States. Hoover was born on January 1, 1885 in Washington, D.C., the son of Anna Marie and Dickerson Naylor Hoover, Senior. The youngest of three surviving children, his older brother, Dickerson, was 15 years his senior and his sister was 13 years older. Dickerson, Senior.

had followed in his father's footsteps and worked for the Coastal and Geodetic Survey; Anna Hoover's uncle had been the Swiss honorary consul general to the United States.

Hoover was born in a two-story house at 413 Seward Square, a neighborhood three blocks behind the Capitol heavily populated by civil servants. As it turned out, J. Edgar would live there for 43 years until his mother died, and he would remain a resident of Washington until his death in 1972. Because of this, Hoover would boast that while he served under eight different presidents, he had voted for none of them, since D.C. residents could not vote for president until the 1964 election, after a constitutional amendment was ratified in 1961.

The single strongest influence on Hoover was his mother, the disciplinarian in the family. In a 1937 article written for the *New Yorker*, Jack Anderson pointed to Annie as shaping J. Edgar's view of the world: "Her domestic justice set up…a pattern of scrupulous regard for law and zeal for punishing wrongdoing, a pattern which as Director his is now trying to impress upon the American mind."

Hoover's youth, while comfortable, was not entirely free of problems. He stuttered as a child and labored throughout his youth to overcome it. He read about various cures, one of which suggested speaking faster rather than slower. He adopted this in an effort to help, but in the process he developed a very rapid speaking pattern that would be a hallmark of him as Director. In order to give himself confidence and further exercise his speaking capability, he joined the Central High School debating team and became a very persuasive public speaker, another skill that would serve him well as the public face of the FBI. Powers later asserted this debate experience was crucial in forming Hoover's character, writing, "It helped develop the combative personality that would fortify him throughout his career. Just as important, it taught him to make a shrewd analysis of both the strengths of his case and its weaknesses."

Hoover was a very strong student and did well at Central High School, excelling at math, Latin and French. He was also athletic. Though he was rejected for the football team because of his height and weight, he joined the track team and helped them win four national championships. Of particular interest to the young teen was the cadet corps; in which he was eventually promoted to Captain of Company A of the ROTC. He took his responsibilities very seriously; his leadership skills were such that he was able to instill in the boys under his charge a respect for excellence. Powers points out the crucial role his time at Central had on his later life: "Edgar carried away from Central a love of competition in a public arena and the conviction that life is, 'nothing more or less than the matching of one man's wit against another.' Throughout his career he loved dispute and looked for opportunities to lock horns with rivals, enemies, even friends ... Hoover liked to fight; most people do not. And so Hoover would eventually wear them down."

Young J. Edgar Hoover

By the time Hoover graduated from High School and embarked on his early adulthood, he was a serious, supremely self-confident young man. Powers wrote that Hoover "took it for granted that his ideas and observations were just as interesting to others as they were to him. He focused on the objective facts of situations, not his emotional reactions. There is a meticulous, exacting quality to his jottings [diary] and a sense of concern about the opinions of others. Because of his dependence on family rather than friends, and because he spent so much time in the company of his elders, he began to act like an adult while he was still a child."

Hoover gave up thoughts of the ministry and instead opted for the law. He was given a scholarship to the University of Virginia but chose to turn it down. Instead, he decided to remain in Washington and attend George Washington University through a work-study program for government employees. To qualify, in 1912 he got a job working as a cataloguer at the Library of Congress. He would remain in the civil service for the next 60 years.

Hoover's career at the Library of Congress had a direct influence on his future career as Director in two specific ways. First, he had the opportunity to see how the Librarian of Congress, Herbert Putnam, operated. Putnam was the 8th Librarian of Congress and considered a master of bureaucratic empire building. Appointed in 1899, he quickly set about to bring order to the library's chaotic collections, going so far as establishing the Library of Congress Classification System and beginning to put the holdings on index cards. Putnam was also able to use his powers of persuasion to get Congress to increase his budget every year he served as Librarian. By the time he "retired" in 1939, Putnam had made the Library of Congress the premier national library in the world.

The second influence on Hoover seems more unusual—his job as a cataloguer. Through the process of referencing and cross referencing each book in the Library by author, title, and subject, Hoover learned the method of organizing large quantities of information in a usable way. Just as a large library would need a central index of its holdings in order to provide the right book to a researcher, a large government office would need a similar index in order to find all relevant information concerning a subject or an individual. Later, when he became director of the Bureau of Investigation, Hoover would apply what he learned from Putnam as a cataloguer to the case files. The system he developed, which involved the indexing of every personal name or organization that appeared in every document that went in an individual case file, remained in use at the FBI with a few modifications until the early 1980s.

Thanks to family connections, namely his uncle William Hitz, Hoover was able to get a job in the Justice Department that exempted him from the draft during World War I. He began as a $900 per year clerk in the files division before being promoted to attorney at $1800 a year. Hoover's rapid rise in the Justice Department was only partly attributable to the influence of his uncle. Frankly, he had little competition; most of the other young men had enlisted, so Hoover was one of the few men available to fill open positions. As such, it was not surprising when his supervisor, John Lord O'Brien, selected him to oversee a group in the Enemy Alien Registration Section, later called the Alien Enemy Bureau.

With the end of the war, concern over German subversives was replaced with concerns over communist subversives. By 1919, the Bolshevik Revolution had spread throughout Central Europe and seemed to threaten the rest of the world. In America, newspaper stories openly worried about a similar revolution in the country. A rash of strikes fed fears that class warfare, fomented by foreign communist forces, would break out at any moment.

For all of the fears over the potential for Bolshevik-inspired violent revolution, when actual radical violence occurred, it was inspired not by the Soviet Union but carried out by an Italian anarchist. Sometime in late April 1919, booby-trapped packages containing dynamite bombs were mailed to 36 prominent political and business leaders, including Attorney General A. Mitchell Palmer. The bombs were sent by followers of the Italian anarchist Luigi Galleani, who was an enthusiastic advocate of the doctrine of "propaganda of the deed," the use of violence to eliminate those he viewed as tyrants and oppressors and to act as a catalyst to overthrow the existing government. His followers intended for the bombs to be delivered on May Day, since May 1 has been celebrated since the founding of the Second International in 1890 as a day of solidarity among communists, anarchists, and social revolutionaries.

Palmer

   While the anarchist's bombs failed to kill any of their intended targets, they succeeded in further increasing the Red Scare hysteria in the country, and other events in the summer of 1919 fed a paranoia about an organized Bolshevik conspiracy intent on revolution. On May 1, 1919, the normally peaceful May Day parades turned violent when large crowds of leftists were met by police and groups of self-described patriots intent on breaking up the demonstrations.

Against this background, Attorney General Palmer struggled to find a mechanism for fighting the "red menace." With the waves of anarchist bombings and racial and labor unrest, Palmer faced pressure from Congress to do something, and in June 1919, he told the House Appropriations Committee that radicals were prepared to "on a certain day...rise up and destroy the government at one fell swoop."

That July, state and federal officers raided an anarchist group in Buffalo, New York, but to Palmer's dismay, a federal judge threw the case out when he found that the anarchists arrested proposed using their free speech rights and not violence to change the government.

Palmer subsequently decided to turn attention to alien radicals, and he became determined to use the existing immigration statutes to deport anarchists, socialists, and communists. To do so, he would need the cooperation of the Secretary of Labor Wilson, who oversaw implementation of the immigration acts. It was Wilson, not Attorney General Palmer, who was authorized to sign arrest warrants and sign deportation orders following a hearing.

The first step was to identify individuals who, because of their immigration status and radical politics, would fall under the statutes. To this end, on August 1 Palmer named a young Department of Justice attorney, J. Edgar Hoover, to head a new division of the Bureau of Investigation. Through the General Investigation Division (often referred to as the Radical Division), Palmer charged Hoover with investigating radical groups and identifying their members. Hoover quickly used his experience at the Library of Congress to develop a detailed process for identifying, indexing, and cross-referencing the names of individuals who could be identified as members of radical organizations. In short order, Hoover and his staff went over lists of subscribers to radical newspapers, membership records, and arrest reports to compile lists of individuals to be subject to deportation proceedings.

On the night of November 7, 1919, selected because it was the second anniversary of the Russian Revolution, Palmer launched a series of raids planned by Hoover in over 30 cities targeting the Union of Russian Workers. The largest raid was in New York City, where dozens of plainclothes and uniformed police officers joined federal law enforcement agents in a raid on the "People's House," the headquarters of the Union of Russian Workers. A reporter for the socialist newspaper *New York Call* described it as "one of the most brutal raids ever witnessed in the city." The arrests cast a wide net, including American citizens, passersby of Russian ancestry, and teachers of night classes using space shared with the Union. Most were released after a while.

Finally, in June 1920, Federal District Court Judge George Anderson in Massachusetts ordered the discharge of 17 arrested aliens. In his decision, he condemned the Justice Department, writing that "a mob is a mob, whether made up of Government officials acting under instructions from the Department of Justice, or of criminals and loafers and the vicious classes."

With this decision, and the end of any prospect that Palmer's raids would be renewed, the First Red Scare effectively ended, and it brought an end to

Palmer's political aspirations. Once touted as a likely Democratic presidential candidate in 1920, he arrived at the Democratic National Convention in July with no chance at winning the nomination.

Ironically, the man most intimately associated with the Palmer Raids today was not its namesake, and his career arc went quite differently. If Hoover had initially been worried about his future career with Palmer gone, it turned out he had little reason to be, because incoming Attorney General Harry M. Daugherty was pleased to find that the files of Hoover's Radical Division contained information on Harding's political opponents as well as radicals. In fact, thanks to his reputation as a nonpartisan bureaucrat who would carry out his superior's instructions without question, Hoover was able to get the job he really wanted: Assistant Chief of the Bureau of Investigation.

In that role, Hoover made himself indispensable to the new boss, William J. Burns. Burns, unlike Palmer, was hardly a taskmaster, giving Hoover the time to take up golf and became more active in his Masonic lodge (he would eventually become a 33rd degree Mason). It's fortunate for Hoover at this time that he had more time, because in 1922 he became the sole support of his mother when his father died.

Burns

Thanks to Hoover's reputation and seemingly straight-laced morals, he was able to avoid the charges of corruption that tarred Burns and another Bureau of Investigation agent, Gaston Means. The Harding Administration was riven with scandals, and the Justice Department was no different. After Harding's sudden death and Calvin Coolidge's assumption of the presidency, Daugherty, Burns, and Means were all removed from office, tried on various corruption charges, and convicted. This left Hoover as the highest ranking official of the Bureau of Investigation.

Unfortunately for Hoover, new Attorney General Harlan Fiske Stone had been a harsh critic of the Palmer raids, but Stone, who had to know of Hoover's role in the raids, nevertheless took the advice of both Assistant Secretary of Commerce Lawrence Ritchey and Assistant Attorney General Mabel Willebrant when they recommended Hoover as the new chief of the Bureau of Investigation. Stone offered Hoover the job of Acting Director, but Hoover recalled later making several conditions of his acceptance of the position: "The Bureau must be divorced from politics and not be a catch-all for political hacks. Appointments must be based on merit. Secondly, promotions will be made on proven ability and the Bureau will be responsible only to the Attorney General."

Stone agreed, and on May 10, 1924, J. Edgar Hoover became Acting Director of the Bureau of Investigation. He would hold the position for the next 48 years.

Hoover was determined to turn the Bureau into the most elite law enforcement agency in the world. With that, he went about making substantial institutional changes. Hoover cut the staff from 441 agents in 1924 to 339 by 1929. All of his energies were focused on making the Bureau a model of good organization and efficiency, to the extent that he actually closed 5 of the 53 field offices and gave back $300,000 of his $2.4 million budget appropriation.

Once he had trimmed the fat by firing agents who were clearly unqualified, Hoover retrained those who remained and raised the hiring standards so from then on all applicants either needed to have law or accounting degrees. Hoover also established a training school for new agents, where they learned various skills and the Bureau's new procedures and code of conduct. Hoover himself developed a system of personnel control, supervision, and accountability that was unrivaled in the government, claiming, "No single individual built the Bureau, but one individual can destroy It." Hoover was determined that that would not happen.

Hoover went to work cleaning house immediately, both to appease the new administration and to shape the Bureau of Investigation to his own preferences. The Bureau had about 650 total employees, including 441 agents, when Hoover took control. He fired all agents he considered unqualified or involved in the corruption brought upon the Bureau by Burns, hired talented young lawmen, and worked to professionalize the Bureau. While these actions went far in establishing a sleek, modern investigative force, Hoover could not help but continue to dabble in political warfare, as he still held his firm belief that the communist threat would destroy America if it were given room to breathe. The General Intelligence Division, rightly seen as a tool of the corrupt administration, was dissolved, but the all-important files, those documents that detailed the Bureau's far reaching and often illegal investigations, remained. Hoover personally kept and oversaw these secret files, which legally should have been made available to Congress and the administration, for his whole life, the details of which were not disclosed until after his death.[9]

---

[9] Ibid., 62.

Tom White was an old-fashioned lawman, the epitome of the frontier sheriff depicted in countless novels and movies. He was born in 1881 in Oak Hill Texas, the son of the County Sherrif, and he grew to be an imposing 6'4 tall, invariably wearing a trademark Stetson throughout his long career. In 1905, he joined the Texas Rangers, and he spent four years pursuing criminals across the Southwest. He spent his time on horseback, armed with a Winchester rifle and a pearl-handled revolver that he could shoot with uncanny accuracy. He gained a reputation as a man who was willing to speak his mind under any circumstances as well as a model of probity and honesty.[10]

---

[10] Texas State Historical Association, White, Thomas Bruce, retrieved from https://www.tshaonline.org/handbook/entries/white-thomas-bruce October 2023.

White

In 1909, he left the Texas Rangers and worked as a special agent for railroad companies, often working undercover and in conditions of great personal danger. In 1917, America joined World War I and White attempted to join the Army, but he was rejected due to having undergone recent surgery. Still burning with a desire to serve his country, he joined the Bureau and quickly became one of its most effective and feared Special Agents.

It would be difficult to imagine a man more different than Hoover. White was a straight-talking, straight-shooting, God-fearing lawman who seemed to be entirely without personal ambition and completely immune to any form of corruption that might lead to personal enrichment. That must have seemed utterly foreign to Hoover, who was driven by intense personal ambition and had never seen a gun fired in anger, let alone arrested a criminal. By late 1924, however, Hoover was running the Bureau and in a tenuous position, so he needed a Special Agent who was completely trustworthy and immune to the potential bribes that any agent sent to Osage County might be expected to face. While many old-fashioned lawmen had been purged from the Bureau after Hoover had taken command (and all female Special Agents had been immediately fired), White remained, and in early 1925 he summoned to an interview with the Director. There is evidence that Hoover didn't particularly like White and viewed what he considered to be White's old-fashioned methods with disdain. Hoover also didn't seem to care for tall agents, as he was rather short.

Regardless, even if he didn't personally care for White, he needed someone entirely trustworthy to take on the investigation in Osage County, and he instructed White to lead the Bureau's investigation into the Osage murders. This was one of the first homicide investigations ever undertaken by the Bureau, and Hoover made it clear that it must not only succeed, but must do so with no hint of scandal or impropriety. White accepted the job and quickly moved to the Bureau's office in Oklahoma City.

When he arrived in July 1925, White's first task was to read the many files accumulated by the Bureau on the Osage County murders. He quickly understood that these represented the visible part of a large-scale conspiracy that must have involved lawyers, guardians, various members of the justice system, and possibly some local law enforcement. He also had to have been aware that some of the people who had previously tried to investigate these murders had themselves been killed. Since this investigation was critical to the Bureau, and also to White's career in it, this was obviously a high-pressure assignment.

Two things quickly became apparent to White. First, the means by which the murders had been committed varied, including stabbings, shootings, poisonings, beatings, and bombings. That seemed to rule out a single perpetrator and instead suggested there was a group of conspirators. Second, some of the murders seemed to cluster around people who had a connection to Mollie Burkhart. As a result, the Burkhart connection is where White chose to begin his investigation.

The first thing White noticed when looking through the files was how much was missing. For example, he noted that the autopsy report on Anna Brown mentioned that her skull had an entry wound, but there was nothing about an exit would. That made it clear that the fatal bullet must have lodged in her skull and should have been an important piece of hard evidence, but those who examined the body denied that any bullet had been found. Some files were also missing entirely – the inquest report on Anna Brown, for example, had been stolen from the desk of the justice of the peace and no copies had been made.

After going through the files, the first issue White faced was whether to undertake the investigation himself. In the past, White had generally worked directly and alone, but he quickly recognized that this case was simply too big for one man. He decided that he would become the public face of the investigation, the man who would talk to the press and deliver updates, but that the actual investigation would be undertaken by a select group of undercover agents.

While Hoover and many new members of the Bureau viewed what they saw as old-fashioned investigators with something approaching contempt (White and others were known within the Bureau as the "Cowboys"), White had little respect for the new breed of agent, whom he regarded as little more than "paper-pushers". What would be needed in Osage County was a group of men tough enough to look after themselves and capable of operating in rough terrain, alone and perhaps for days at a time. Every member of the investigating team would have to operate undercover and with cover stories strong enough that they would be able to withstand scrutiny.

White had been given the authority to choose the team that he would work with, and these agents were recruited from amongst the Cowboys in the

Bureau. Three of the agents chosen were white. A 56-year-old former sheriff arrived in Osage County playing the role of a retired cattleman. Another former Texas Ranger, a man who seemed to relish assignments that involved personal danger, became a rancher looking to buy property in Osage County. Another agent, a former insurance salesman, opened an office in Fairfax and played the role of an insurance agent. The last member of the team was the only one with Native American heritage, John Wren, who had recently almost been dismissed from the Bureau for his unwillingness to file detailed reports. To White, he was an invaluable member of the investigating team who would be able to talk to Osage in a way that white members could not. Wren arrived in Osage County as a traveling Medicine Man who claimed to be searching for lost relatives.

The two agents posing as cattlemen were directed by White to try to get close to William Hale, Mollie Burkhart's father-in-law and a man White suspected of being involved in the murders. The insurance salesman visited homes in Osage County, ostensibly touting for insurance business but in reality collecting important gossip. Tom Wren attended tribal gatherings at which he was able to speak with the Osage.

Arrests and Trials

As information began to flow into the Bureau office in Oklahoma City, White gradually began to build a picture of the murders in Osage County and a clear pattern began to emerge: almost all of the victims were either Osage who owned headrights or those who had tried to investigate what had happened to them. It seemed certain that money was behind the murders, but just who was involved?

The Bureau's agents focused their investigation on the murder of Anna Brown. The undercover agents had found witnesses in the town of Ralston who claimed to have seen Anna Brown in a car on the evening she disappeared, well after the time that Bryan Burkhart claimed that he had dropped her off at her home. One of the witnesses, a local farmer, told investigators that he had been sitting outside the hotel on Ralston's main street with a group of people when a car pulled up right next to them. In the car was Anna Brown, whom he knew, and he spoke to her briefly before the car pulled away.

Other people who had been present corroborated this account, and, when the witnesses were asked who else was in the car, they all claimed that the driver had been Bryan Burkhart.

However, at the inquest into Anna's murder, Bryan had given evidence that he had dropped her off at her home in Fairfax between 4:30 and 5:00pm, and that he had not seen her after that. The sighting in Ralston took place later in the evening, so if the accounts witnesses gave were true, then Bryan Burkhart had lied at the inquest. Subsequent investigations revealed other sightings of Bryan, Anna, and perhaps another man in a car in various parts of Osage County as late as 3:00 a.m. the following morning.

However, the investigation was made more complicated by the presence in Osage County of private detectives employed by the Burns Detective Agency, founded by none other than former Bureau Director Burns. These men made little effort to investigate the murders and instead seemed to do their best to impede the efforts of White and his team. One agent in particular, named Pike, went out of his way to try to undermine the credibility of anyone who seemed willing to speak with the Bureau's investigators, including a small-time criminal named Kelsie Morrison who had agreed to work for the Bureau. Pike was arrested soon after on a charge of armed robbery in Tulsa, and Bureau agents questioned him. Anxious to have the charges against him dropped, Pike told the agents that he had been hired by Hale, not to investigate the murders, but to make sure that the Bureau didn't look too closely at his nephew, Bryan Burkhart. As a result, the Bureau's agents became even more interested in Bryan Burkhart, while also starting to wonder whether there was a larger conspiracy that somehow involved William Hale.

The investigation then looked at the murder of Henry Roan, who had been found in his car, shot in the head, in February 1923. Hale was the beneficiary of a life insurance policy that Roan had taken out that would pay $25,000 in the event of his death. When the policy was examined, it showed signs that it had been tampered with, and most notably, dates seemed to have been changed. Before the policy would become active, Roan had to undergo a medical examination, and Hale had taken him to a doctor in Pawhuska. The doctor was interviewed and recalled asking Hale jokingly, "What do you plan to do, kill this Indian?" Hale had seemingly responded in jest, "Hell yes![11]"

The case against William Hale was growing, but it was entirely circumstantial – the agents had not found a single piece of physical evidence or identified a witness who could conclusively connect William Hale or his nephews Ernest and Bryan Burkhart with any of the murders. It was also clear that Hale had powerful friends in the sheriff's department and the judicial and political system across Osage County, so making a case against him would be very difficult. Bureau agents made contact with a number of criminals serving time in prison who seemed willing to talk in exchange for a reduction in their sentences, but the leads they provided led nowhere. Two men had been named by these informants as being responsible for the bombing of the house of Bill and Rita Smith: Henry Grammer, a bootlegger and long-time friend of Hale, and Asa Kirby, an explosives expert and bank

[11] Cited in David Grann, *Killers of the Flower Moon: The Osage Murders and the Birth of the FBI*, 2017.

robber. As it turned out, Grammar had died in a car crash in June 1923, and Kirby had been shot dead during an attempted robbery a few months later. The owner of the store that Kirby had attempted to rob had been tipped off and was waiting with a shotgun, and the person who had given him the tip was none other than William Hale. In retrospect, this certainly could have been a convenient way of getting rid of a potentially inconvenient witness, but once again, the evidence against Hale was circumstantial.

It was another imprisoned criminal who would finally provide the evidence that the Bureau needed. Burt Lawson was serving a sentence for armed robbery in the Oklahoma State prison, and he made it known that he had information about the Osage murders that he would be willing to trade for a reduction in his sentence. He was interviewed by agents, and what he told them was dramatic. He had first been approached by Ernest Burkhart, who asked him if he would be willing to blow up the house of Bill and Rita Smith (Lawson had previously worked as a ranch-hand for Bill Smith). He refused, but he was then approached by Hale, who offered him $5,000 to do the job. Again, he refused, and shortly after that, he found himself in prison facing a murder charge after the death of a local fisherman. Hale visited him in prison and offered to pay for his defense if Lawson would assist with the bombing. Lawson agreed.

Lawson gave a detailed account of how he was secretly released from prison while he accompanied Hale and Ernest Burkhart to plant the bomb. He was then returned to prison and was later acquitted on the charge of murder, as Hale had promised.

On October 24, 1925, Hoover finally received the news he had been waiting for when White reported that he finally had a confession that directly implicated William Hale and Ernest Burkhart in three of the Osage County murders. By that time, Mollie Burkhart was seriously ill, and White and others believed that she was being poisoned by Ernest Burkhart or William Hale. If she died, Ernest would inherit all her headrights and would suddenly become enormously wealthy.

In December 1925, warrants were issued for the arrest of William Hale and Ernest Burkhart for the murders of Bill and Rita Smith and their maid,

Nettie Brookshire, and the two men were arrested the following month.

At first, the case against Hale and Burkhart did not look strong. Hale denied any involvement in the murders and claimed that he had an alibi for the time of the explosion in Bill Smith's house – he had been in Texas at the time, where he had received and signed for a telegram. If that was true, then it would indicate that Lawson had lied and the Bureau's case would collapse.

Then, dramatically, White received a message from Ernest Burkhart in prison. He was willing to tell everything, but he would only talk to White. White went to see Burkhart in prison, and Ernest gave a full confession. He admitted to playing a role in the explosion in the Smith home, but he said that he had done this only at the instigation of "Uncle Bill," William Hale. He also told White that Hale had arranged the murder of Henry Roan in order to benefit from the life insurance policy. He named the killer that Hale had hired for this murder as John Ramsey, a known criminal who lived in Osage County. A warrant was quickly issued for Ramsey's arrest. At first, Ramsay denied any involvement in the murder of Roan, but after intensive questioning by Bureau agents, he finally confessed to the killing and claimed that he had been paid by William Hale.

William Hale's claimed alibi for the time of the explosion at the Smith home proved unreliable, and as the case against Hale was built, Mollie Burkhart was removed from her home and taken to a location where she could be guarded. Almost immediately, her mystery illness subsided, and she began to make a full recovery. William Hale meanwhile, despite being confronted with the growing evidence against him, continued to deny any involvement in any murder. It was clear that this case would be decided in court.

The pre-trial hearing began in March 1926 in the State Courthouse in Pawhuska, and it quickly became obvious that Ernest Burkhart was terrified of his uncle and would not be a reliable witness. He recanted the confession he had given to White, claiming it had been forced out of him, and he became a defense witness, testifying that he had no knowledge of the explosion at the Smith home or the murder of Henry Roan. When John Ramsey also seemed less confident about the confession he had given (he claimed in court that he had "never killed anyone"), the case against William Hale was in danger of falling apart.

In late May 1926, the trial of Ernest Burkhart for the murder of Bill Smith began. At first, Burkhart continued to deny involvement in any murders and once again claimed that he had been threatened and coerced by the Bureau's agents into giving his confession. The court heard testimony from Kelsie Morrison, who, in May, had confessed to killing Anna Brown. He claimed that he and Bryan Burkhart had taken Brown, who had been drinking, to the creek where her body was later found, and Morrison shot her in the head. Morrison claimed that he had been paid by William Hale to carry out the murder, and he also described what he knew about the explosion at the Smith house. After hearing Morrison's testimony in early June, Ernest Burkhart dramatically changed his plea from not-guilty to guilty as charged. On June 21, 1926, Ernest Burkhart was sentenced to life imprisonment with hard labor.

That was a triumph for the Bureau, but it still left William Hale free amid claims he was completely innocent. At the end of July 1926, the trial of William Hale and John Ramsey for the murder of Henry Roan began in a courthouse in Guthrie in Logan County, Oklahoma. Despite the evidence against him, Hale seemed confident and continued to proclaim his innocence. The defense attempted to blame Ernest Burkhart for the murder of Henry Roan, and despite the fact Ernest Burkhart gave evidence to the court against Hale, the Bureau still had no hard evidence that conclusively proved Hale's guilt. In August the jury reported that it was unable to reach a verdict. The judge was left with no option but to dismiss the jury and schedule a new trial. When Bryan Burkhart was tried for the murder of Anna Brown soon after, the jury in that trial was also hung and a new trial had to be ordered.

A 1926 picture of Hale and Ramsey in the middle with U.S. marshals next to them

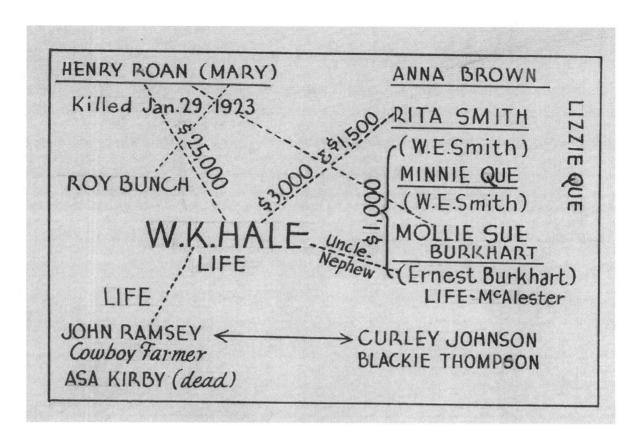

**A document from the case piecing together
Hale's ties to suspects and victims**

The case so carefully built by White and his team
of agents seemed in danger of collapsing, but the
Bureau also began investigating claims of bribery in
the trial of William Hale. One witness who had
given evidence at that trial told investigators he had
been approached by Hale's defense attorney, Jim
Springer. The witness claimed that Springer had
offered him money to lie in court and, when he
refused, threatened to have him killed if he testified

against Hale. The second trial of William Hale and John Ramsey for the murder of Henry Roan began in October, and this time, the Bureau also had the task of protecting witnesses and members of the jury from threats and bribes.

Before Hale and John Ramsey were tried again, other trials had been taking place in Osage County. Bryan Burkhart was tried a second time for his part in the murder of Anna Brown, but he was found not guilty. Then Kelsie Morrison was tried on the same charge. By the time he came to court, he had recanted the confession he had given in May and claimed that he had nothing to do with Brown's murder. However, Bryan Burkhart, now immune from prosecution in the case since he had already been found not guilty, testified against Morrison and gave a full and dramatic account of the murder of Anna Brown. He told the court that he and Morrison had taken her to a remote location, knocked her on the head, carried her down close to the creek, and then Morrison shot her in the head. Keslie Morrison was found guilty of Anna Brown's murder and sentenced to life imprisonment.

The second trial for William Hale and John Ramsay began in October and lasted just eight days. After a single day for deliberation, the jury announced on October 29 that it had reached a verdict: William Hale and John Ramsey were guilty of murder in the first degree. Both men were sentenced to life imprisonment.

The successful convictions of Ernest Burkhart, Kelsie Morrison, William Hale, and John Ramsey vindicated the Bureau and J. Edgar Hoover, who ensured the trials' results were widely covered across the country.

The Aftermath

In the 1930s, the Bureau began to work with a nationally syndicated and extremely popular radio show, *The Lucky Strike Hour*. Originally a music and variety show, the series began to feature dramatic reconstructions of major criminal investigations, and Hoover and the Bureau became involved with providing case information. One of the first episodes to feature this new format covered the Osage County murders, and the show concluded with a statement that the criminals involved in the criminal conspiracy proved "no match for the Federal Agent of Washington in a battle of wits.[12]" The reputation of the Bureau's agents being indefatigable, determined, and incorruptible would be established and fostered personally by Hoover over the next half century.

In 1932 the Bureau of Investigation was renamed the United States Bureau of Investigation, though it retained the same duties and responsibilities. The following year, it was attached to the Bureau of Prohibition and became the Division of Investigation, but in 1935, it became an independent agency of the Department of Justice and was given the name under which it would become world-famous: the Federal Bureau of Investigation (FBI).

Hoover remained the FBI's leader for almost 50 years until his death in 1972. Under his long tenure, the FBI grew from an obscure part of the Department of Justice into one of the United States' largest law enforcement and criminal investigation agencies. It remains involved in counter-espionage, opposing organized crime, and undertaking

---

[12] Cited in David Grann, *Killers of the Flower Moon: The Osage Murders and the Birth of the FBI*, 2017.

extensive (and sometimes questionable) surveillance of American citizens. It can be argued that it was the widely publicized success of Bureau agents in Osage County that provided the initial success that led to its subsequent growth. It's certainly true that a failure in Osage County, or perhaps hints of some new scandal, might have caused Hoover and the Bureau serious problems. Instead, Tom White and his team were able to break a major conspiracy and to see members of that conspiracy jailed for their part in the Osage County murders.

Ultimately, that success led to the Bureau's version of events being accepted as the true story. According to the Bureau, the Osage County murders were planned and ordered by William Hale and carried out by his nephews and others. It certainly seems reasonable to accept that Hale was guilty as charged of the murders of Bill and Rita Smith, but there remains a wider mystery that was never addressed by the agents. For example, Hale was never implicated in the murder of Barney McBride in Washington or W.W. Vaughan, who was murdered as he rode a train from Oklahoma City to Pawhuska. Both men were investigating the Osage

County murders, and their investigations were far more widespread than the killings of the immediate family members of Mollie Burkhart. Likewise, Hale was not implicated in the murders of Charles Whitehorn, William Stepson, Joe Bates, George Bigheart, and other Osage. Modern historians now believe that the number of Osage victims might be as high as 100, and in retrospect, it is likely there was a far wider conspiracy in Osage County that went well beyond William Hale and his family members.

What is clear is that local law enforcement, the justice system, the coroners, and the justice of the peace appeared to be completely disinterested in investigating the deaths of Native Americans in Osage County in the 1920s. It is altogether possible that some deaths attributed to natural causes were actually murders, most likely committed in order to gain control of headright payments, but nearly a century later, it's highly unlikely any of these suspicious deaths will now be investigated. To date, nobody else has ever been prosecuted for any of the other murders.

In his 2017 book *Killers of the Flower Moon*, author David Grann examined the evidence related to these unsolved murders, and he believed the conspiracy included the involvement of a bank president, members of local law enforcement, members of the justice system, and others appointed as headright guardians. As a result of his critically acclaimed work, the FBI looked at new evidence in the case of the murder of Charles Whitehorn, but concluded that it was insufficient to justify a new investigation. Grann's contention that William Hale was "not an anomaly" is difficult to dispute.

Tom White left the Bureau soon after William Hale's conviction. His effective work in Osage County had attracted the attention of the Assistant Attorney General who was trying to find a new warden for the oldest federal prison in America, Kansas' Leavenworth Prison. There had been allegations of brutality and corruption in the prison, a new warden was needed who could restore its reputation, and White seemed to be the ideal man for the job. In the fall of 1926, he took up his new position, and, in the kind of bizarre coincidence that no fiction writer would dare include in a work, two of the first inmates who arrived at the prison after his arrival were William Hale and John Ramsay. White was badly wounded during an escape attempt by prisoners in 1931 and was subsequently moved to the less stressful position of Warden of La Tuna Federal Correctional Institution in Texas. After his retirement from the prison service, White served on the Texas Pardons and Parole Board. He died in 1971 at the age of 90.

Although he had been sentenced to life imprisonment, William Hale was released on parole in 1947 after serving 20 years, as was John Ramsay. Hale worked on ranches in Montana and Arizona after his release and died in 1962 at the age of 87. Ernest Burkhart was paroled in 1937 after serving just 10 years of his life sentence, though he was barred from returning to Oklahoma. In 1940, he was caught burgling a house in Osage County and returned to prison. He was paroled again in 1959, and in 1966 he applied for a pardon, citing his cooperation with the Bureau's investigation. This was granted, after which he returned to Osage County, where he died in 1986 at the age of 92.

Mollie Kyle divorced Ernest Burkhart during his trial for the murders of Bill and Rita Smith. She remarried in 1928 and continued to live in Osage County. She died there in 1937 at the age of 50.

All the while, the Osage continued to receive headright payments after the reign of terror ended. In order to prevent further murders, Congress passed a new law in 1925 that prohibited a non-Osage individual from being able to inherit a headright payment. The Department of the Interior continued to administer the trusts from which headright payments were made, but some Osage complained that these trusts were mismanaged, leading to the disappearance of funds and the loss of interest payments. In 2000, the Osage filed a lawsuit against the Department of the Interior, and in 2011, the Osage received a settlement of $380 million, the largest settlement awarded to any Native American group in American history. Many Osage continue to receive headright payments, and oil exploration and drilling are still taking place in Osage County, providing employment and economic benefits for its residents.[13]

---

[13] The *Osage Nation* website, retrieved from https://www.osagenation-nsn.gov/news-events/news/did-

The murders in Osage County were emblematic of a dark chapter in American history. In theory, the Osage had the same rights as any other citizen, but as the legal system and murders made clear, that was hardly the case. During the trial of William Hale, one local newspaper carried a quote from an Osage tribal leader who complained, "It is a question in my mind whether this jury is considering a murder case or not. The question for them to decide is whether a white man killing an Osage is murder - or merely cruelty to animals.[14]"

Online Resources

<u>Other books about Native American history by Charles River Editors</u>

Further Reading

David Grann, Killers of the Flower Moon: The Osage Murders and the Birth of the FBI (2017), Knopf-Doubleday Publishing Group

Bill Burchardt, "Osage Oil," The Chronicles of Oklahoma 41 (Fall 1963)

---

you-know October 2023.

[14] Cited in Tulsa World, *Racism, greed during oil boom created environment for Osage murders*, October 7th 2023.

Doherty, Jim (2004). Just the Facts: True Tales of Cops & Criminals. Deadly Serious Press. p. 192. ISBN 9780966753479. Archived from the original on 2019-03-21.

Franks, Kenny Arthur (1989). The Osage Oil Boom. Oklahoma Heritage Association. p. 180. ISBN 9780865460751. Archived from the original on 2019-03-21.

Hogan, Lawrence J. (1998). The Osage Indian Murders: The True Story of a Multiple Murder Plot to Acquire the Estates of Wealthy Osage Tribe Members. Amlex. p. 282. ISBN 9780965917414.

Kennedy, Deanna M.; Harrington, Charles F.; Verbos, Amy Klemm; Stewart, Daniel; Gladstone, Joseph Scott; Clarkson, Gavin (2017). American Indian Business: Principles and Practices. University of Washington Press. p. 248. ISBN 9780295742106. Archived from the original on 2019-03-21.

Grann, David (2017). Killers of the Flower Moon: The Osage Murders and the Birth of the FBI (First ed.). New York: Knopf Doubleday Publishing

Group. ISBN 9780385534253.

Hess, Janet Berry (2015). Osage and Settler: Reconstructing Shared History through an Oklahoma Family Archive. North Carolina: McFarland. p. 232. ISBN 9781476621173. Archived from the original on 2019-03-21.

Willard H. Rollings, Unaffected by the Gospel: Osage Resistance to the Christian Invasion, 1673-1906: A Cultural Victory (2004), Albuquerque: University of New Mexico, 2004

Louie McAlpine, "Osage Medicine: Ancestral Herbs And The Illnesses That They Treat", Grayhorse Indian Village, Scope Publications, 1998.

Terry P. Wilson, The Underground Reservation: Osage Oil, Lincoln: University of Nebraska Press, 1985.

Sister Mary Paul Fitzgerald, Beacon on the Plains, Leavenworth, Kansas: Saint Mary College, 1939

William White Graves, The Annals of Osage Mission, 1934

Gibson, Arrell M. 1972. Harlow's Oklahoma

History, Sixth Edition. Norman, Oklahoma: Harlow Publishing Corporation.

Printed in Poland
by Amazon Fulfillment
Poland Sp. z o.o., Wrocław
25 October 2023